NOTTINGHAM
PAST & PRESENT

This elegant doorway in the Castle grounds doesn't lead anywhere. It was formerly part of a hotel on Friar Lane.

BRITAIN IN OLD PHOTOGRAPHS

NOTTINGHAM
PAST & PRESENT

GEOFFREY OLDFIELD

SUTTON PUBLISHING LIMITED

Sutton Publishing Limited
Phoenix Mill · Thrupp · Stroud
Gloucestershire · GL5 2BU

First published 1999

Reprinted in 2002

Half title page photograph: Middle Hill before
Broad Marsh Centre was built.
Title page photograph: The Fox and Grapes
public house on Southwell Road was better
known as the 'Pretty Windows'. Its name is
now Peggers.

British Library Cataloguing in Publication Data
A catalogue record for this book is available from the
British Library.

ISBN 0-7509-2296-6

Typeset in 10.5/13.5 Photina.
Typesetting and origination by
Sutton Publishing Limited.
Printed in Great Britain by
J.H. Haynes & Co, Ltd, Sparkford.

The houses on Wellington Circus were demolished as they were on part of the site of the Playhouse.

CONTENTS

Much of the property between Canal Street and Broad Marsh was demolished in the 1930s. The site was used for a time as a bus station.

The Park Tunnel (see page 80).

INTRODUCTION

In my previous book in this series, *Nottingham Yesterday and Today*, published in 1995, I used black and white photographs of Nottingham which I had taken mainly in the years 1955 to 1975. I accompanied these with photographs taken as far as practicable from the same standpoint as the earlier ones. From 1939 to around 1955 the main building activity in the city had been the erection of the new houses, mainly on estates on the outskirts of the city, together with the essential amenities on new estates such as shops and schools.

The older parts of the city therefore had remained largely unchanged for up to sixty years. From 1955 onwards the gradual clearance of many of the older houses, a process which had commenced in the 1920s and 1930s, took place. This process also involved the demolition of other kinds of buildings to enable satisfactory redevelopment of the areas. The same attention had to be given to the traffic problems caused by the growth of the use of motor vehicles. My earlier book illustrated how the city changed in that period, not just the centre but also parts which had formerly been separate districts.

This book now tries to take the story one stage further. Most of the photographs of *Nottingham Past & Present* have been reproduced from colour slides which I started to take some thirty or so years ago. Again, I have accompanied them with photographs of the scenes today. These show particularly the older parts of Nottingham, which was a small borough in acreage until the second half of the nineteenth century. They reflect the way Nottingham has altered, as many other towns have done, owing to technological, social and cultural changes.

Most of the photographs are of parts of the city which are less than a mile from the Old Market Square. They reflect the considerable amount of capital investment which has taken place in recent years, and in fact is still taking place.

The Town Arms is now The Aviary, the Globe Cinema has gone and Turney Brothers Ltd's leather works has be
converted into flats.

CHAPTER ONE

AROUND TRENT BRIDGE

For a thousand years travellers coming to Nottingham from the south have passed over Trent Bridge. The first bridge was ordered to be built in 920 by King Edward the Elder. A later medieval bridge with many small arches lasted until 1871, when it was demolished. The first glimpse of Nottingham Past which today's travellers have is a surviving arch of the old bridge in the middle of a traffic island, shown in this photograph.

The new bridge, opened in 1871, has only three arches over the river. By 1926 it was no longer wide enough for the increasing traffic and it was doubled in width. In recent years alterations both north and south of the bridge have taken place, again to cope with increased traffic.

Turney Brothers' leather works had been established in about 1860 at the end of London Road but the building in this photograph with the name on it was built in 1911. The firm had been founded by Sir John Turney, twice Mayor of Nottingham.

The chimney and other buildings have been demolished, but the main building has been converted into living accommodation and the site renamed Turney's Quay.

The view of the north bank of the River Trent where the Nottingham Canal joins it included part of Turney Brothers' building.

Part of the new Turney's Quay development can be seen on the left of the present view

This view of Turney's 1911 building is taken from the end of Arkwright Street. The cobblestone feature in the road replaced flower beds.

The main difference to the leather works building is the treatment of the windows. The cobblestone feature has been replaced with a shrubbery and ornamental lamps.

The buildings adjoining the main Turney's building had been demolished, opening up new views.

A new road gives access to the houses erected on the cleared site. Some of them back on to Nottingham Canal.

A small garden between Turney's leather works and the River Trent was at one time the departure point of paddle steamers.

The garden has been redesigned with new trees, and Nottingham Forest football ground has had new stands built to provide an all-seat stadium.

THE MEADOWS

Until 1952 Trent Bridge was wholly within the City of Nottingham, because of the irregular line of the boundary with the county. Since then the centre of the river has been the boundary, so only the northern half of the bridge is now in the city. Beyond lies The Meadows district, so called because it was part of the ancient common fields established when the Anglo-Saxon town of Nottingham came into being on a sandstone cliff 1 mile north of the River Trent. A road linking the old bridge with the town was named the Flood Road and the meadows would often be flooded in winter. This was the only road into the town until the 1860s, when building on the meadows started and a new road – Arkwright Street – was made. The new buildings, including many houses, were to be subject to periodic flooding, culminating in what it is hoped was the last time in 1947. Since then remedial works have prevented serious floods, although the photograph here, taken twenty years ago, shows that wet winters can cause the river to rise above the level of the embankment.

The Globe Cinema, erected in 1914, stood at the end of London Road, on the right of the picture, and Arkwright Street.

Boots Institute, the black and white half-timbered building on the left of the picture, is the only building shown on the picture above which survived when The Meadows was re-developed.

London Road, seen here from near the Greyhound public house, still had buildings on the left-hand side, and two-way traffic was in operation.

The buildings have been demolished and a grassed bank with trees planted to minimise traffic noise for the new houses. The Greyhound is now DC's Bar.

Most of the buildings on Arkwright Street were demolished as part of the redevelopment scheme. St Saviour's Church had its vicarage looking on to Glebe Street.

Glebe Street has disappeared, and this section of Arkwright Street has been pedestrianised and re-named Arkwright Walk.

This view of Arkwright Street looking in the opposite direction shows how the gradual demolition of houses caused shops to close before they too were demolished. St Saviour's Church can be seen behind the bus.

The no. 43 bus, which replaced the trolley bus route with the same number, can be seen in the previous picture. It ran from Bulwell Market to Trent Bridge. Buses through the new Meadows now run along some streets such as Bathley Street and Wilford Grove.

Some of the industrial buildings in the Meadows survived where they did not affect the radical new street pattern. This is one of them on Crocus Street.

The main difference in this view of Crocus Street today is that the remains of the railway viaduct were demolished a few years ago.

Waterway Street had a number of terraces which ran through to Crocus Street. In this picture some new industrial buildings had been built on the renamed Meadows Way.

A new building erected ten years ago now adjoins the industrial building which was retained. The short street connecting Crocus Street is Mabel Street.

Bertram Street was entered through an archway from a footpath off Crocus Street, and was flanked by the rear of factories on London Road.

The street has entirely disappeared, but some of the London Road factories can be seen behind the new buildings.

Kirkewhite Street was divided in two by Arkwright Street. This photo shows the western half with Healey Street and other streets on the left-hand side. The former railway bridge can be seen crossing Kirkewhite Street.

Bridgeway Hall had been rebuilt before the main redevelopment of The Meadows. The junction box and wall on the right form a useful marker on the pedestrianised shopping precinct.

Cromford Street curved round from Kirkewhite Street to Arkwright Street. The Porters Rest public house was conveniently close to Arkwright Street station. The adjoining building was a woollen waste dealer's.

Like so many other streets Cromford Street has disappeared, and forms part of the site of new dwellings on Blackstone Walk.

This picture was taken after the house on Annesley Street had been demolished and Sheriffs Way was being constructed.

The large building at the corner of Waterway Street West has been renamed Karlsruhe House in honour of Nottingham's 'twinned' city.

Mundella School was erected in 1897 and named after A.J. Mundella, President of the Board of Education and a former Town Councillor of Nottingham.

The Secondary School later became Mundella Grammar School but was demolished in 1985. The dwellings erected on the site are called Mundella Court.

CHAPTER THREE

NOTTINGHAM CANAL

In 1796 the 15-mile canal from Langley Mill and the Cromford Canal connected the town of Nottingham with mineral deposits, including those of coal in Derbyshire. Within the borough, as Nottingham was still at that time, the canal ran below Nottingham Castle, then as far as the Flood Road (later called London Road) to the east. It then turned south and ran parallel with the Flood Road to the River Trent. This was a great boost to Nottingham's trade until the railways came.

Today the only remaining stretch of the canal within the city extends for about a mile and a half before joining the Beeston Canal. It has seen numerous changes, especially when the railways came to Nottingham. The Carrington Street bridge over the canal is only half a mile from the city centre and the view from the bridge has changed considerably in the last few years. Further changes to both the west and the east have taken place and are still in progress.

The small bridge shown in the photograph here is on the towpath of the canal a few hundred yards from Carrington Street, but this view from the south has only been made possible because of recent developments on both sides of the canal.

The entrance to the former railway goods yards had a gate which was attached to the original brick piers from the first railway station.

The original brick piers have been retained as part of the entrance, alongside the canal towpath, to the magistrates court.

The view from Carrington Street Bridge in 1964 showed, on the right-hand side, some of the buildings used when the canal was used for freight. The railway buildings on the left-hand side were separated from the canal towpath by a wall.

From the same viewpoint today can be seen the new buildings which have been erected and the refurbished former British Waterways warehouse.

The building shown here was a warehouse alongside a part of the canal used for loading by the boats of Fellows, Morton and Clayton.

The warehouse was demolished when the former building adjoining Fellows, Morton and Clayton was converted into a canal museum, which has recently been closed.

uildings on the south side of Canal Street, between Wilford Street and Carrington Street, had other buildings
ttached that backed on to the canal.

ll the buildings shown above have been demolished as far as the former Stevex warehouse. This has been converted
to a public house, and another new one has been erected next to it. Both have outside areas facing the canal.

In this picture part of the old railway buildings on Carrington Street are in the top right-hand corner.

Both banks of the canal have been improved and a new footbridge connects them.

ter the buildings on the east side of Wilford Street had been demolished, this view of those on the west side
uld be seen temporarily.

e new *Evening Post* building has been erected on the cleared site, and the British Waterways former warehouse
s been renovated.

All these buildings on Wilford Street have been demolished to form part of the site named Castle Wharf.

This view of the *Evening Post* building shows the entrance at the corner of Canal Street and Wilford Street.

The entrance to the former railway goods yard on Wilford Street had a weighbridge.

On this site the magistrates court and Nottinghamshire Archives buildings have been erected. A road connects with the Inland Revenue building on the other side of Wilford Street by an underpass.

This view from Wilford Street, over the railway lines, shows the cleared railway lands and the rear of buildings on Castle Boulevard.

Train passengers coming into the Midland station from the west can see the new Inland Revenue buildings, Howard House, a design won in competition by the Michael Hopkins Architectural Practice.

Taken from the south end of Castle Bridge Road, this picture shows the partly cleared site of the railway lands.

On this site a number of retail establishments have created an out-of-town shopping centre with parking space.

At the west end of Castle Boulevard are several streets of houses which back on to the canal, including Alderney Street and Petersham Street at the far end of this picture.

Cecil, Chippendale and Marcus Streets remain largely unchanged, but new development at the far end includes Castle Gardens.

t its eastern end, Nottingham Canal turned south running parallel to London Road. Nearby was Eastcroft Gas 'orks, and this photograph shows the site of the demolished gasometer.

n this site a new industrial estate has been created, with trees to soften the visual aspect.

The canal also extended an arm eastwards between Boots' Island Street site and the former railway line on a viaduc

The whole of the Island Street site has been cleared, as has the railway viaduct, giving new views beyond the form railway station entrance.

gh Level railway station stood on the bridge that crossed over the southern arm of the canal.

ne bridge and viaduct have been demolished and the eastward arm of the canal filled in. The canal has been ade into a pool with a viewing platform.

From the viewing platform, over the cleared site can be seen the industrial buildings on Pennyfoot Street.

This scene has changed already, as the new BBC building has been erected and work has commenced on other schemes

CHAPTER FOUR

AROUND THE CITY CENTRE

For centuries, until the second half of the nineteenth century, Nottingham's market-place was the central feature of the borough and the built-up part of the town only extended a short distance around it. When the open fields were released for building, and after the borough was extended to bring in adjoining parishes, the town started to expand. Today the city, as it became in 1897, extends 5 miles northwards from the Old Market Square but only for a mile or so from most of its southern boundary. It is not therefore the geographical centre, but it remains the focal point of much of the city's aspects of life today. Although no longer the hub of Nottingham's shopping it remains the vibrant heart. Many of the city's bus services pass through or terminate at the city centre, and its former market-place has been laid out as an open space with flower beds and fountains flanking the ceremonial processional way leading to the Council House. The photograph shows the scene in March 1997 when the Queen visited the city as part of its celebrations of being granted that title one hundred years earlier.

Nottingham's Council House, completed in 1926, has come to be regarded as the symbol of the city. The thoroughfares surrounding it have been altered from time to time and the roundabout shown in this picture has been removed.

The square now has new bus shelters and on the left of the picture can be seen a modern sculpture, Quartet.

The Bell Inn has recently been judged to be the oldest building in the Old Market Square.

Recent alterations to the pavement now mean that patrons can enjoy their refreshments outside, weather permitting. A link with Nottingham's past is shown on the plaque.

Opposite the Bell Inn was one of Nottingham's oldest department stores. A disastrous fire in 1995 meant that its successor was closed for some years.

The newly restored building is now in use again.

This view, taken from under the dome of the Council House, shows the cleared site of the Black Boy Hotel on Long Row.

The entrances to the Arcade were open until a few years ago when they were fitted with large glass doors.

When Long Row East was pedestrianised a gazebo was erected. As it was open on all sides it was only used occasionally.

A less draughty new structure is now used as a shop.

Near the top of Market Street was the
Scala Cinema, which had formerly been
a music hall but was converted into a
public house.

The Robin Hood Tavern was replaced by a
new building as part of the redevelopment of
the Pearson's store site.

Clumber Street has been pedestrianised and several of the buildings have been demolished, as has the one in this picture.

The replacement has incorporated a motif on the apex similar to the one on the previous building.

St Peter's Square just south of the Old Market Square was at one time a bus terminus. In this picture a West Bridgford UDC bus was about to turn right into St Peter's Gate.

The Square has now been incorporated into the pedestrianised route of Albert Street and Lister Gate.

St Peter's Church Walk once connected St Peter's Gate with Low Pavement, by way of Church Street. When the latter was closed a footbridge was erected, and this quiet oasis had a fountain.

Recent alterations at the rear of St Peter's Church mean that there is no through way to Low Pavement and the fountain has gone.

When some of the buildings on Exchange Walk were demolished it was possible to see the side of the Flying Horse Hotel on Peck Lane.

The hotel has been mostly demolished but part has been incorporated in Flying Horse Walk shopping mall. A glimpse of the Peck Lane windows and gables can be seen from St Peter's Gate.

The building on the left of this picture was the Flying Horse Hotel garage.

The garage was demolished in 1987 and the new building on the site is the St Peter's Gate entrance to the shopping mall. The adjoining building has not been altered apart from the ground floor.

The cobbled Pepper Street connected
St Peter's Church Walk with
Bridlesmith Gate.

St Peter's Church Walk and Church
Street have been built on and
Pepper Street is now a cul-de-sac,
much shorter than when it was a
thoroughfare.

This was the site of the Gate Inn on Bridlesmith Gate after the public house had been demolished. The Anglo Saxon ditch would have been on or near this site.

The new public house erected on the site of the Gate Inn is named The Fountain.

CHAPTER FIVE

FROM THE OLD MARKET SQUARE TO THE CASTLE

The Normans built the first castle on the commanding rock and sandstone site soon after the conquest of 1066. The castle's history for the next six hundred years is part and parcel of the town's story. When the Duke of Newcastle erected his ducal mansion on the site in 1679 it opened up a new chapter of Nottingham's history as the gentry started to build fashionable houses in the streets leading from the castle, as the Duke insisted on calling it still. The nineteenth century saw the burning of the Castle in 1831 and its renovation and opening of its first museum and art gallery in 1878.

A visitor to the Castle today can see something of Nottingham's past in the grounds and in the museum. Not the least of its attractions are the views of the city and parts of the surrounding countryside. The photograph shows a convenient stone seat half way up the steep slope on the east side of the Castle. The bench incorporates part of a fireplace from the old castle

In 1976 extensive excavations of the medieval castle were carried out, and this picture shows part of the walls and a tower under the green.

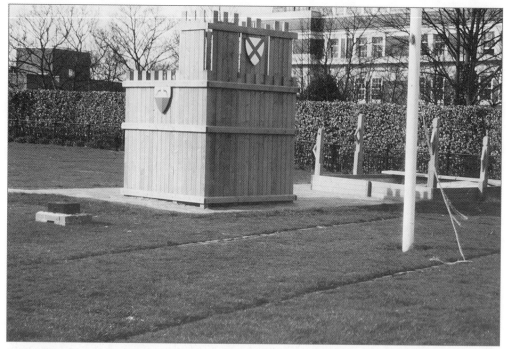

Although the remains had to be covered over again lines of stones now indicate the layout of the part of the castle underneath the green. Children's play equipment has been designed to reflect medieval architecture.

This view over the Castle Green shows the General Hospital's nurses' home and the Trent Wing, which was erected in the 1960s.

Taken from the same viewpoint, the main difference is the disappearance of the Trent Wing with the redevelopment of the General Hospital site.

The walk in the Castle grounds overlooking Castle Road revealed the changes which had taken place nearby. This view shows the rear of the houses on Castle Gate and Walnut Tree Lane.

Now one can see the reconstructed Severn's building from Middle Pavement, the rear of the Costume Museum and part of People's College of Further Education.

The first building on the south side of Castle Gate appears to have a flat roof.

It now has as its neighbour the reconstructed Severn building. Castle Road has cobblestones as it is not now a through street for traffic.

This view reveals that the apparent flat roof in the picture on p. 61 is not what it seems. It also shows the rear of the Georgian buildings on Friar Lane.

New buildings at the end of Castle Gate have transformed the view.

Looking south-east from the south front of the Castle the former buildings north of the British Waterways warehouse could be seen.

The partially completed Castle Wharf and the magistrates court now occupy the centre of the picture.

To the west, the buildings of the Queens Medical Centre seem surprisingly near, 2 miles away. In the foreground are the as yet undeveloped former railway lands.

Because of the fall of rock on the south face, it is not possible to take a photograph from exactly the same point as the picture above.

Newdigate House, often referred to as Marshall Tallard's house, has survived for 300 years. The turret roof of Mortimer's House on Castle Road can be seen on the left.

The new buildings on the now pedestrianised part of Castle Gate do not have the elegance of Newdigate House.

Before Maid Marian Way was made St Nicholas' Rectory, designed by Watson Fothergill, adjoined the church. The gate piers to a small garden can also be seen.

The central reservation of Maid Marian Way has been planted with trees on the site of the old rectory, in an attempt to soften the visual impact of the high-rise buildings.

The view to the south-east from St Nicholas' Churchyard formerly had a view of industrial buildings with a tall chimney.

The buildings have now been converted into offices, which do not need a coal-fired furnace with a chimney.

One of the earliest buildings to be erected at the bottom of Maid Marian Way was People's College, which took its name from the mid-nineteenth-century school on the Ropewalk.

Subsequent alterations to the College have reduced the view of the Castle.

The demolition of the buildings on the east side of Stanford Street revealed views of the shops on Carrington Street, which went to form part of the site of the Broad March Centre.

These buildings on Stanford Street are part of the new buildings on Lister Gate.

Greyfriar Gate, seen here from the traffic island on Canal Street, joined Lister Gate and Carrington Street at the Walter Fountain, named after John Walter, MP for Nottingham.

Broad Marsh Shopping Centre can be seen on the right with a multi-storey car park on the left.

CHAPTER SIX

NORTH & WEST OF THE CASTLE

Immediately north of the Castle is Standard Hill, so called from King Charles I's action in erecting his standard there as a symbol of the start of the Civil War in 1642. Until the middle of the nineteenth century it remained outside the jurisdiction of the borough, and when the General Hospital was opened in 1782 the ground on which it was built, Derry Mount, was described as 'near Nottingham'.

To the west of the Castle the land was converted to a royal park for the king to use for hunting when he was in residence. After the demolition of the medieval castle and the granting of the site to the Duke of Newcastle, the land of the former royal park was also transferred to him. In the nineteenth century it was developed as a planned site for the erection of large houses which was named simply The Park, a name it still retains.

Whilst the then Duke of Newcastle was a minor the estate was administered on his behalf by trustees, one of whom was William Ewart Gladstone, Prime Minister three times. One of his hobbies was felling trees and the plaque on Tunnel Road contains a section of one which he felled on a visit to The Park.

A contrast in architectural styles on St James Terrace and Rutland Street – which ranged from elegant Georgian houses to a nineteenth-century warehouse and a mid-twentieth-century car park.

The warehouse has now been replaced by the Rutland Square Hotel.

The left-hand side of upper St James Street had been cleared of buildings and the site left as an open space, revealing the flank of the former warehouse of Griffin & Spalding's.

The open space has been retained, now giving the side view of the Rutland Square Hotel.

When the General Hospital was still in use an iron bridge crossed over Postern Street to link the hospital buildings on Mount Street.

The demolition of part of the General Hospital included the bridge, but the pier with a statue in a niche remains.

When the nurses' home on Standard Hill (formerly the site of St James' Church) was demolished, the hospital chapel could be seen.

The Jubilee Tower remains, in use for offices with a public house on the ground floor, while the chapel has been converted into a restaurant and new offices have been erected.

The Pay Bed Wing of the General Hospital, at the junction of Park Row and The Ropewalk, was demolished in 1998.

New dwellings with a splendid view from the upper floors have been erected on the site.

Demolition of all the buildings between Park Row and Cumberland Place revealed new views of Regent Street, Park Row, the Albert Hall and the spire of St Barnabas' Cathedral.

Mount Street car park adjoins the building on Park Row which is one of a new group stretching down to Maid Marian Way.

A temporary use of Granby Street, seen here from Park Row, was a bus station.

Granby Street was incorporated into Maid Marian Way and new buildings have been erected on Park Row.

From The Ropewalk and Newcastle Drive the ground sloped steeply down to the valley. A house on Newcastle Drive had a garden on the slope; the ruined buildings were formerly stables.

New dwellings have been built on the site, and Tennis Drive's name reflects the existence of the excellent courts between it and Tattershall Drive.

The appropriateness of the name of this road, Tunnel Road, can be appreciated from this view.

Today the tunnel cannot be seen from the same viewpoint although it is still there, coming out on Derby Road.

It is not many years since a horse could be seen grazing less than three-quarters of a mile from the Old Market Square, on Lincoln Green.

One of two such circular open spaces in The Park, Lincoln Circus is now laid out with paths and seats.

The end gable of this former stable block in The Park is unchanged from the days when the inhabitants were mainly 'carriage folk'.

The building itself shows the changes of this century, having been converted into living accommodation with a garage.

CHAPTER SEVEN

THE LACE MARKET

The Saxon settlement of Nottingham, on a steep cliff above the low-lying marshes, was a comparatively small site. Over the succeeding centuries it emerged as the administrative heart of Nottingham, and after the Normans founded the French Borough alongside the Castle it became the English Borough. The two eventually coalesced but the original borough remained as the main seat of town government until the nineteenth century.

In the eighteenth century, in the same way as did the area adjoining the Castle, the old borough had elegant houses and mansions built on it. When the advance of industrialisation forced the gentry to seek more rural dwellings, the houses often became the homes and warehouses of the hosiers when their trade expanded. In the nineteenth century, when the lace industry overtook hosiery, the lace manufacturers similarly started to occupy the former hosiery warehouses. These in the main proved inadequate for the growing lace trade and older houses were demolished to make way for purpose-built, often elegant warehouses. The decline of the lace industry in the twentieth century left the Lace Market, as the area had been called since about 1850, in a run-down state.

Advertisements on the window of the warehouse on Broadway, above, indicated some of its variety of products. The windows have now been replaced with clear glass.

The rejuvenation of the Lace Market in the last thirty years has been a noteworthy chapter in Nottingham's long history.

The site on the left of this photograph had been the site of the medieval Town Hall.

Garners Hill urban park has been created on the cleared site. The retaining wall on the right-hand side enables a strip of land adjoining the former High Pavement Chapel to be used for parking.

The derelict buildings at the rear of High Pavement Chapel had been used as the High Pavement School until it was moved to Stanley Road in 1895.

The renovated buildings were used as offices and the chapel became the Lace Hall for a time. The sign Pitcher & Piano reflects its present use as a public house and restaurant.

The original brickwork of 3 and 5 High Pavement was revealed when stucco covering was removed.

After renovation, the building is now the Museum of Lace.

The elegant wrought-iron gate at the Shire Hall
led to a side entrance for judges when courts
were held.

The Shire Hall is now the Museum of Law, and
the gate now gives access to a café.

Commerce Square housed a warehouse which was built on top of an existing building on Cliff Road, Renovation involved uncovering a lower floor.

The whole building, down to Cliff Road, has been converted to apartments and an extra storey has been added.

The buildings at the bottom of Hollowstone, including a former post office, had become very dilapidated in the 1960s.

Once the buildings had been cleared, the City Council grassed the area and planted trees to give a more attractive appearance to an entrance to the Lace Market.

The Old Rose Revived public house on Bellar Gate ceased to be used for that purpose in the 1920s but survived as storerooms for another sixty years.

When the building was demolished the site was incorporated into the adjoining disused burial ground to form a grassed area, which has a beautiful display of crocuses in early spring each year.

On the west side of Fletcher Gate next to the Cross Keys public house is the former lace warehouse at one time occupied by Splendour.

Queen Victoria would not be amused by the name the Old Vic, given to a public house converted from the former lace warehouse.

On the east side of Fletcher Gate, opposite the Cross Keys, was another public house, the Windmill.

Fletcher Gate was widened on the east side, which involved the demolition of the Windmill, revealing the walls of buildings on Pilcher Gate which have been given a face-lift.

The demolition of warehouses between Stoney Street and St Mary's Gate was intended as an extension of Barker Gate but was used as a surface car park.

Plans were changed and a new building on the site houses a car park and offices.

The Adams Building on Stoney Street, opened in 1855, had a rear entrance on St Mary's Gate with the fine lettering 'Adams & Compy'.

The building has been extensively renovated for New College and the rear entrance has been retained. The lettering has been gilded and the name plates which indicated the former multi-occupation have been removed.

The former theatre on St Mary's Gate was badly damaged in an air raid in 1944, and the remaining site with the front wall housed an electricity station.

The wall has been well preserved as part of the Bridge Housing development in Halifax Place.

One of the St Mary's burial grounds off Barker Gate, which were made in the nineteenth century, had been disused for many years and has been converted into a small rest garden.

Some of the buildings on Maiden Lane, at the rear of the rest garden, have been rebuilt.

This view of Warser Gate from its junction with Stoney Street shows the former chapel at the corner of Bottle Lane and Fletcher Gate.

The chapel has been demolished, as have some of the old buildings beyond St Mary's Gate.

The Old Angel public house on
Stoney Street can be seen at the
end of Warser Gate viewed from
Fletcher Gate.

The buildings on the right in the
earlier picture have been demolished
and the site is now used as a car park.

Some of the buildings on Woolpack Lane were demolished to form a new road linking Barker Gate with Hockley. This gave archaeologists an opportunity to investigate medieval developments.

The new road is named Belward Street and is a busy one-way thoroughfare.

Seen from the eastern end of Canal Street, the lace warehouses around Trivett Square were a prominent landmark.

The new dwellings and offices erected on the site have excellent views to the south.

The former Town Arms public house on Hollowstone was demolished after it was damaged by a fire about ten years ago.

The site has been developed along with the adjoining Trivett Square.

The cleared site of the Town Arms revealed the existence of the sandstone cliff at the bottom of Hollowstone.

This shows the southern aspect of the development; the eastern aspect is shown on page 101.

Malin Hill was an ancient footway up the side of the High Pavement cliff. It runs from Commerce Square to Plumtre Square, and the former Town Arms flanked Short Stairs.

The new development incorporates the steps of Short Stairs up to Short Hill.

Short Stairs had a number of old buildings on both sides.

The new development retains the old steps at the bottom of Short Stairs.

he Plumtre Hospital on Plumtre Square was rebuilt in 1823 when the street was known as Red Lion Square.

he residents of the hospital were rehoused to new flats a few yards away on Canal Street, and the old building is eing converted to offices.

When the buildings on the north side of Fisher Gate were demolished the rock face at the rear was exposed.

New housing accommodation has been built on the cleared site.

Patrick's Roman Catholic Church was in the centre of this view of the junction of Canal Street and London Road.

his view of the redevelopment of the site shows the new Plumtre Hospital flats and Trivett Square prior to the
cent alterations.

A power station for Boots' Island Street premises was built at the end of London Road.

The power station, now part of Nottingham's district heating plant, is one of the few remaining buildings today at the junction of London Road and Canal Street.

The demolition of Allen's property at the junction of London Road and Lower Parliament revealed some of the industrial site of the Island Street complex.

The second new building on the Island Street site has been erected. The picture also shows the Stag and Pheasant public house a short time before it was demolished.

This 1930s Art Deco-style garage was at the junction of Barker Gate and Parliament Street.

The site of the garage and other adjacent buildings is now undergoing a complete transformation to form the new Ice Centre.

CHAPTER EIGHT

NORTH OF PARLIAMENT STREET

U ntil the 1830s there was very little development north of Parliament Street, because the open fields could not be built upon until opposition from the burgesses was overcome. The Lammas Fields were the first to go, with Regent Street, Oxford Street, Wellington Circus, St Barnabas' Cathedral and the Albert Hall making their appearances. The much larger open fields on both sides of Mansfield Road, the Sand Field and the Clay Field, were both developed after an Act of Parliament was obtained in 1845. The Sand Field, on the east side and extending to Forest Road, saw the establishment of a middle-class suburb, with its profusion of streets named after literary figures – Shakespeare, Goldsmith, Dryden, Addison. Municipal development followed with the University College and the Guildhall.

On the east side of Mansfield Road below Woodborough Road, the workhouse had been built in the 1830s and between it and Parliament Street was a squalid area of early nineteenth-century houses. Both these were to disappear in the 1890s with the building of the new railway and Victoria station. The closing of the railway line and the demolition of Victoria station created the site of the Victoria Centre. For twenty-five years the section north of Union Road lay undeveloped and formed an unofficial nature reserve. Most of it has been built on as an extension to the Victoria Centre. Further east, the St Ann's area was the size of a small town, mainly with working-class dwellings cheek by jowl with industry. The last thirty years have seen considerable changes in parts of these areas, although some still remain as reminders of a more leisurely age.

Following the completion of Maid Marian Way, Derby Road was made a one-way street. This involved the demolition of most of the buildings in this picture.

New buildings erected included those on Toll House Hill, joined by a section bridging over the street.

At the bottom of Wollaton Street was an old building with white stucco, which was the Gellestrope Almshouses.

Now a one-way street, in the opposite direction to Derby Road, Wollaton Street has new buildings including a car park with totem pole-like features.

Around Wellington Circus were a number of former dwellings, which have been partially demolished in thi picture.

The cleared site was used for the erection of the Playhouse, a modern structure of unusual design.

his was Nottingham's first electricity generating station. It remained in use as the main office of the electricity epartment after a more modern generating station was built in the 1920s.

This site is now occupied by a car park attached to the Moat House Hotel.

On Wollaton Street was another group of almshouses. Hanley Street took its name from the charity.

When the almshouses were demolished, new ones at Bilborough were incorporated with the replacement of the Gellestrope charity. The site has been partially built on, but gives views of Talbot Street.

This part of Goldsmith Street was between Burton Street and Theatre Square.

All the buildings were demolished and the site was used for the erection of the Concert Hall.

Further along Goldsmith Street, past Chaucer Street, had been a number of buildings including the Eye Infirmary. On the other side were Victorian houses.

On both sides of the street new buildings for Nottingham Trent University have been erected.

The Midland Design Centre, at the junction of Mansfield Road and Peachey Street, was erected to give developers information on designs of buildings and their furnishings.

After the Design Centre closed, Sandfield House was used for additional magistrates courts until the new ones were built on Carrington Street. The building has been given a face-lift and is to be used as a Voluntary Action centre.

The BBC occupied York House on the right of this picture. The other building, formerly the Roebuck Hotel, was also known as the BBC – but this stood for Bobby Brown's Café.

The café has been demolished and new premises erected on the island site backing on to York Street.

The building which formerly stood on Lower Parliament Street, at the corner of Beck Street, had been destroyed by fire, revealing views of what had been Parker & Booth's shoe warehouse.

New premises have now been erected on the cleared site, restricting the previous view.

The building with the patterned brickwork was on Chaucer Street, adjoining the rear of a factory on Talbot Street.

The new buildings on the site include the Nottingham Trent University Law School and the Belgrave Centre.

These houses on Mansfield Grove were typical of those built on the Sandfield in the 1860s: they had become dilapidated and were demolished.

New houses have been erected on the cleared site, and the part of Mansfield Grove which led off Peel Street has been built over.

In the days when circuses had performing animals the elephants led a procession along Mansfield Road to the Forest.

The buildings in the background were formerly the Bluecoat School but are now part of an International Community Centre.

Some of the buildings on the right-hand side of Woodborough Road had already been demolished, revealing a view of Emmanuel Church before it too disappeared in 1971.

New houses have been built on both sides of Woodborough Road.

Robin Hood Chase only had houses on both sides formerly, but when St Ann's was redeveloped a shopping centre and library were included.

The new building in the centre of the photograph has a turfed roof, which helps to conserve heat.

This building at the corner of Lower Parliament Street and King Edward Street was erected in the 1920s, but had its name changed a few years ago.

Nostalgic memories of its former use were revived when its original name, the Palais de Danse, was partially restored.

The Nottingham newspaper offices were erected in 1897 and extended along South Sherwood Street and Burton Street thirty years ago.

All of the properties extending to Trinity Row have been demolished, and have opened up new views pending redevelopment.